# A Prayer
## for
# Torn Stockings

*Poems*

# Suzanne O'Connell

## GARDEN OAK PRESS
### RAINBOW, CALIFORNIA
gardenoakpress.com

Garden Oak Press
1953 Huffstatler St., Suite A
Rainbow, CA 92028
gardenoakpress@gmail.com
(760) 728-2088

First published by Garden Oak Press   April 18, 2016

ISBN-13:   978-1530028641

ISBN-10:   1530028647

Printed in the United States of America

To my husband,
JEFF O'CONNELL,
all my love and gratitude

# CONTENTS

Humans are a lot like
refrigerators.
The light only goes on
when someone takes the time
to open the door and look inside.

# A Prayer

## for

# Torn Stockings

## Poems

## Suzanne O'Connell

GARDEN OAK PRESS

# Hairdresser

I cried today when you cut my hair.
It was my first haircut in ten years.
The style was fine,
you didn't do anything wrong.

You see, hair grows six inches a year.
The part you cut
was the last part he touched
before he died.

# My Life as a Meteor

A melon dropped from the sky last Thursday.
I ran over to the patch of lawn where it landed.
I touched it all over
to see if it was real.
I couldn't tell if it was a
Crenshaw,
Canary,
Casaba,
or Cantaloupe.
I didn't want to touch it *too* much,
or taste it for that matter.
It could be radioactive
after its plunge through space.

The fallen melon reminded me of my childhood.
Unpredictable things happened all the time.
Like that one day when I was 13,
I noticed new pills in the medicine cabinet.
The label said they were for my mother
and they were for
*GESTATION AND LACTATION.*
I didn't know these words so I looked them up:
> *Gestation is the process*
> *of being carried in the womb*
> *between conception and birth.*

Then I had to look up *womb*,
but I was getting the picture.
Shortly after that, my brother appeared
in a basket on the couch.

I didn't understand most of what went on in my life.
Forks and grandparents disappeared.
Dad sprayed whipped cream in his face.
I was failing arithmetic.
Full bottles of wine appeared in the bushes.
Our cat Tommy ran away and moved in with another family.

I was a lot like that melon.
Solitary,
heavy as a bowling ball,
falling through the silent language of the stars
to an unknown landing.
People touched my net-like skin without asking.
They sniffed my stem end
to figure out if I was one of their tribe,
they shook me to see if my seeds were loose.

People scratched their heads and couldn't explain
the mystery that was me.
Then the melon cracked open
and I fell out.

# Seducing Mr. Rogers

You will want to know that his cardigan was the color of Irish chalk,
chalk once dug up in County Cork
by a peasant's hand from a hill of peat.
The peat that remained on the grassy hill was later burned
for warmth in the drafty cottages.
But sometimes the peat on the grassy hill
was known to spontaneously combust into flames.
After a time, the fire would ebb and smolder
under the surface for many years.
Like a similar element of the natural earth,
I too was burning under the surface with a smoldering fire.

I knew two things must first happen.
His glasses must be removed and placed on the tiny
window sill above our heads.
I glanced through the spectacles for a moment,
hoping to capture the world as he viewed it,
through the two transparent planes.
I noticed a fingerprint smudge on one lens
that I cleaned off using the lace of my cotton slip.
I folded the spindles back and set them
carefully down.
His eyes looked unfocused and watery.
His eyes were the blue of an early morning cloudless sky.
The blue of a rabbit's eye.
The blue of a hard spearmint candy.
The eyes were not looking at me, but outward,
displaced,
disowned,
like a priest's eyes deep in prayer.
Later the eyes would close but not yet.

The thing I knew must happen next was the mussing of his hair,
hair like dried shellac,
hair trapped all its life in a stiff crust.
Hair that dreamed of freedom.
I created a gray and black thunderstorm
of abandon with my hands.

6

You will want to know that he stood very still
as I unzipped the cardigan,
unzipping slowly as I was afraid the sudden cold draft
would upset his delicate equilibrium.
We were standing in the cloakroom,
so I hung the cardigan on a brass hook
alongside all the others.
They were hung like human skin discarded in battle.
There was a smell in the cloakroom,
a combination of fear, cardamom seeds and brisk aftershave.
I breathed deeply in order to remember the smell.

You will want to know that the obstacles were many.
The complexity of the layers of clothing
would have discouraged a less determined person,
but my hands were confident.
My mind had many times rehearsed what my hands were doing.
I felt like a lace maker who was taking one stitch
after another in order to create a masterpiece.
After the cardigan,
his red and blue nautical tie was unfastened
by reversing the overhand knot.
Then, starting from the tail and moving
up to the throat,
the small pearl buttons of his white oxford shirt were undone.
Next the ribbed sleeveless undershirt
that a young boy could have worn in an orphanage
was lifted overhead.
Lastly, I removed his pressed and cuffed tan pants
and his chaste undergarment.
The pile of clothing lay at our feet.

His mouth moved only once,
making a small but noticeable change.
Was it pleasure?
A protest?
A prayer?

continued

You will understand that I can't tell you everything.
But it was very quiet in the playroom except for the toy train
that ran on schedule around the ceiling track.
The train was traveling nowhere in particular,
but the clacking percussive sound
of the metal wheels on the wooden track
sounded a bit like breathing
as I stood there in the cloakroom,
holding my breath and waiting.

# So Many Spiders

Every day there is a spider in the bathtub,
waving his hairy legs around.
Legs like a folding measuring stick,
too complicated for the small package.

Every day I enclose the spider in a white tissue
and carry my bride,
my prom date dressed in white,
my spider ghost,
to the nearest plant on the porch.

Today it occurred to me for the first time
that maybe it's not a bunch of spiders after all,
but *one persistent* spider.

Maybe it wants to be part of our household.
Maybe it wants a little red sweater on cold days,
to be up on the bed with the rest of us
watching TV at night,
to be under the down comforter.

Maybe he loves being carried in
that envelope of white tissue
from room and room,
my stowaway,
my cuddler,
my little spider baby.

# Hymns and Hems

I thought hymns
and hems
were the same.
I pictured God
bent underneath
the table lamp,
holding his needle
and thread,
stitching up
those beautiful chords,
the ones
that shook the walls
of the church
every Sunday.
I pictured God
stitching his perfect
overcast stitches,
to hem the trees
and rivers
and mountains
of the world,
so they wouldn't trip.

# That Kind of Girl

She was the kind of girl who took her own pulse all the time,
three digits on her artery, fingering the frets on her neck like a guitar.
When others were around, she pretended
she was brushing aside a strand of hair.

She was the kind of girl who couldn't say the words
tit-mouse or ball-cock or matriculate.
She couldn't say breasts either, but said blossoms.

She was the kind of girl who was buttoned all the way up.
She only ate fish that swam wild, were never
caught in nets. She underlined with a ruler.

Yet at midnight, she removed her clothes and climbed the ladder
to the rooftop, where she sat eating saltines.
Then she danced like she was cardboard coming unglued,
and she sang Serbian folk ballads to the stars.

You've heard the old saying about the still pond
that is deep and full of vitamins?
Or the one about the bushel basket that hides rumors and kisses?

Well, she was that kind of girl.

# A Prayer for Torn Stockings

Bless the torn stockings,
and the sinking ship.
Bless the nights of sin,
and the hard of hearing, who miss a lot.
Bless the left-handed ones,
because they can be somewhat peculiar.

Bless the bloated,
and the forgotten on the dirt road.
Bless the film star
and the digger of the ditch.
Bless too the wandering rabbit,
wandering in the blurred eye of night,
and may our little friend be cloaked by darkness.

Bless the table, spread with abundance,
and also bless the potato in a child's pocket.
Bless the inventor of the zipper
and bless the warm bread stuffed with nuts and plums
for the sweetness upon our tongue.

Blessings on this night,
blessings stitched as fine as lace underthings
strewn over the trees.
Blessings on all of us,
as we stand here in our torn stockings.

# The Armadillo

Ancestral thug, King Arthur of the sloth world,
I salute you!

My knight in leather pantaloons,
I sing your praises.

You have made ugliness hot.
You know how to throw your man-muscles around,

how to impress the ladies with your slick sword.
You are never lonely, the girls flock to you.

You can inflate your insides and swim across rivers!
What prowess, my leathery hero.

Just one thing I can't understand.
How do you bed your Guinevere?

How do you push aside your thick armor
to reveal your tender places?

Oh my macho rabbit in a turtle's shell,
I have known so many men like you!

# Reclaiming the Forest

I call her my jungle.
Black hair creeps over her body
like the nightshimmer vines crawl
over the forest floor.

Her pale canopy is covered
by the black thatch.
I hide the photo of her in a bikini
when guests visit.

I insist she pluck,
bleach, shave,
have the pulsing light treatments.
But the creepers continue to creep.

The growth threatens to consume her
like a choked tree in the jungle.
It begins to choke us as a couple.
It keeps me from her like a chastity blanket.
I can't look at her.  I refuse to touch her.

Later, she meets a new man and I lose her.
He loves the beauty she is on the inside.
He doesn't notice the black vines
that cover her body.
He reclaims the forest that I had plundered.

# My Little Hand

I grew my skin myself.
My mother – she didn't play fair.
She was a stack of charred papers.
My daddy was a floating head in front,
hands on the wheel,
while mother re-applied
her lipstick.

There was something alarming
that I couldn't name.
On my birth certificate, I was named
as my own mother.
A real switheroo!
But, I wasn't laughing.

I took my little hand and showed myself
around.
This is what mothers do after all!
They point and say, tree.
They point and say, shoe.
They point and say, be careful, red light.

I pointed with my own little finger.
I taught myself to spit gasoline
and to smell the smell.
I kissed mortal sin.
I kissed mortal combat.
I kissed my Uncle John's blind eyes.

I wandered around my town,
pointing at things,
teaching myself,
and holding my own little hand
while I crossed the busy streets.

# Down Below

Down past the crumb coat,
down past the primer,
down past the stained nude nightgown,
down the old wooden ladder,
down to the sparks,
down even below the sparks,
down to where the rain collects
in the cold basement,
down past the kitten with ringworm.
Turn left at the first grey room.
Turn left again past the cluttered bedroom.
Then, there in the kitchen,
with the mellow light shining down
on the table covered by a plaid tablecloth,
you will find a little girl
sitting next to her grandmother.
They are slicing dates,
inserting a walnut in each one,
and rolling them in sugar.

# A Girl Drowning

"Keep the knees closed and the mouth shut,"
the grownups instructed.
But my ears – like my mouth – had been stapled
shut.

On the bank,
the grownups laughed and ate sandwiches,
waiting for me to die.

Above me, the moon exploded
and the trees smelled like sweet
camphor and open perfume bottles.

I felt a flame inside my body.
I wanted life.
I wanted to sizzle with life.

"We're still waiting," they yelled across the river.
"You will have to speak louder," I yelled back.

# One in a Million

Last night in a dream
my father whispered to me
I was one in a million.
Or, maybe I overheard him
bragging to someone else,
as fathers sometimes do.

I don't want to overthink this,
because I was smiling
and felt so proud when I woke up.
But I do wonder if he meant
it as a compliment?
Maybe he meant that,
*statistically* speaking,
my personality type is rare,
and meant it
not in a complimentary way.

My father never gave compliments.
He had been a Marine
stationed in the South Pacific
on an aircraft carrier.
He had two bone-on-bone hip
replacements.
He still holds the record for the most
consecutive tournament games of tennis
ever played.
Compliments made a kid soft and weak.

I've held on to the only compliment
I can remember.
He said I sang along with a song
on the radio
in my own *true* voice.

I don't want to overthink this,
but maybe he meant he appreciated
my own true voice,
the real me,
and not the toady little
phony I had become.

# Hamel's Weekend

Hamel sings unitones in church.
He wears a unitard, unzipped to the navel
to reveal his hairy chest.

Hamel goes to the Silent Movie Theater
to watch old movies, the ones with the
cowboys wearing tight white pants.

Hamel feeds the gang of swans in the afternoon,
feeds them bits of Bremer Klaben
and Neufchatel cheese.

Hamel sometimes puts his toe in the water.
The swans swim over, thinking it's
a tidbit of something novel.

Hamel holds still so he can feel
the nibble of the swans on his big toe.
Life is so delicious, Hamel thinks.

# The Volunteer

I'm just fine except for the falling paper.
A curtain of scraps falls before my eyes.
An animated river.
A looping waterfall.

I didn't mention the falling paper
to the nice lady
during my exit interview.
Nor the dark edges around my vision.
I didn't mention the weight I've lost.
Or the sleeping issue,
waking every hour or so,
tangled and sweating.

But I'm fine.
The paper bits I see are small.
They are not the full sheets
that covered the cars and the streets
of lower Manhattan
like tainted snow,
lifting with each breeze,
pulsing,
before settling back down.

One piece of paper said:  $82^{nd}$ floor,
please help me.
I think it was addressed to me.
I found it on a parked Toyota
covered with white powder,
but I was too late to help.
I also couldn't help the man who
tried to wash the dust out of his hair
when it turned to concrete.
Or the child who asked if there is
Jazzercize in heaven.
I couldn't help the firefighter who,
well I can't go into it.
Or my coworker who was asked to leave
because she began to think she was
with the FBI.

Compared to them, I'm fine.
Really.
If I can get the falling paper to stop,
I'll be okay.

# The Shore of You

Was there a cry when I was born?
Not from you, of course.
I meant from me.

Was there
a healthy lung-cleansing?
A howl or two?
Was there a cry declaring my arrival
on the new moon?
The moon where I pitched my flag
as I washed up
on the shore of you.

Was there a cry as I slid
in to home plate?
Was I safe or out?
Was there a cry to celebrate
my long journey
from the nethers
to the new homeland?

Was there a cry
from that bed
at Mercy Hospital?
Or did I wait,
even then,
to see what you expected?

# If You Blink

A brick might be thrown at your Volkswagen.
Oh, my generation of mud!
The nights here can be so hot!
I'll tousle your hair if you gaze upon the welts on my thigh!

Remember when every night was summer?
Remember when my whistle was sharp?
Remember the days when we ate cheese all night,
in the bathtub with Willie?

I was once the teacher and now it seems I am the pupil.
Sick laughter and bile rise, my girl!
Come sit on the glider with me and breathe a while.
Let me tell you what I have seen.

# Lentils and Crackers

After three other seasons,
summer is a gift.
After summer, we might die.

In winter, the eggs and spinach will be lost.
We will be left with lentils and crackers,
and our toes for walking.

Put on your keen hat, my dear,
tell your mother we might be aliens.
I'm watching, girl, so make it brief.

It's time to wander,
to walk to the edge of the river together,
with the dark tribe of just you and me.

# My Own Lemon

I want my own lemon.
I want my own towel,
not one already moistened
by your shower.
I want my own blue coffee cup,
not one with the baby's milk in it.

As a mother, nothing belongs to me.
My body is on call.
I can't eat what I prefer.
I can't walk outside by myself.
My house is a toy emporium!

That's why last night,
on our date night,
when you reached over
and took meat from my plate without asking,
I stabbed your hand with my fork.
I'm sorry about the blood on your new shirt,
my dear.

# The Sultan's Nose

"It's called the Sultan's Nose," she said.

She handed me a brochure that described the new acquisition.
Her green apron sported the arboretum logo.
Her name badge read: GRISELDA.

Sticky leaves reached out to pinch me.
Branches lurched, made menacing faces.
Stinging nettles bit my hand and fumed in the corner.

"Why is it called the Sultan's Nose?" I asked.

The plant was orange, the color of a ripe persimmon.
It's spines bristling up the stalks like a cactus.
But there was no rounded protrusion like a nose.

"Why do you think I gave you a brochure?" Griselda replied.

Funny how it doesn't matter if it's a plant or a human
doing the scratching and biting,
it still leaves a sting.

# How to Cook and Serve a Husband

A new husband may have a high altitude.
In the beginning, one layer may form a hard crust,
or be too thin,
or form a hump in the middle.

But, ask yourself,
how often have you quickly obtained perfection?
It is always important to plan ahead!
Never forget: "the stomach is the seat of courage."

In the cottage kitchen or the great house
on the hill,
it is important to try to prepare
a dainty and appropriate meal!

If, however, something burns,
or hardens before you spread it,
or is not an attractive combination,
never fear!

New husbands can benefit from tender endearments.
Feed their tender hearts if not their hungry stomachs!
The prudent wife who fails in the kitchen
may choose to extend one of the following
affectionate bon mots:

You are my lightening biscuit
You are my plump sweetbread
You are my nut bar
You are my hot molasses
You are my golden glow
You are my apple bun
You will forever be my royal educator!

# The Secret Life of Beans

Chinese long beans are the kittens of the garden.
They creep with silent paws along the earth
until they reach a patch of sunshine where they
stretch and pull vitamins out of the light.

Rolande beans are the dapper ones.
Fastidious in all matters of appearance,
they become as straight as chimneys
when visitors arrive
and they love having their picture taken.

Red noodle beans are the comedians.
They practice their standup routines
and hope that children will visit
as they are the only ones who ever laugh.

The Spanish Miraldas are the sexpot beans,
especially in the heat of summer.
So out of control are they,
some gardeners resort
to covering them with blankets.

Maybe when beans arrive at your house,
they will hang out in a hot pan
with butter and sliced almonds.
Maybe they will bathe in a cream sauce
with crackled onions on top.

Maybe when beans arrive at your house,
you will tip your ear down
and they will tell you the story
of their miraculous childhood
in the garden.

# Origami

I fold myself in half,
My thumbnail smooths down the long crease.
I fold myself in half again.

I'm a neat package,
one that could contain a secret word,
money, or a photograph.

I lift one corner of myself,
fold back, and repeat on the other side.
I look like a nun's hat

from the New Hebrides.  I don't even know
where the New Hebrides are,
but I'm struck by the word He Brides.

I open myself flat,
like a bride on her wedding night.
I survey the creases of my folding.

The creases remind me of architecture,
of rooms I have lived in,
of my newlywed apartment.

With a small fold in the middle,
I make a beak and then a neck.
I fold myself back into the neat package.

I admire my wings,
my wise expression,
my is neck bowed,
either in resignation or humility.

Those who look may see a swan bride
in her wedding gown.
They will never know
that I am folded inside.

# Dear Sugar Daddy Jesus

I didn't pray to get things off my chest.
I prayed to get results.

Dear Deep Pockets Jesus, I prayed.
Please fill up my empty meat with
golden sunlight.
Please make one of the Calderone brothers
like me. I'd prefer Chris, but Phil would be okay.
Please turn my hair blonde and straight.
Please let me pass arithmetic.
When will I get breasts?
I am waiting.
Will you please hurry!

Jesus was so wise. He was my brainy Heart Throb.
I drew pictures for him
and hid them behind my dresser.
The pictures were mostly of him on the cross
with the stabbed chest, thorns and nails.
I wanted him to know we were a team,
and if he was suffering, I was too.
He never said thanks.
He never said anything.

Dear Honeycomb Jesus,
can you make me rich?
And can you stop all the arguing
in this house?
Can you make my sister run away?
Please let me live at grandma's.

Dear Glazed Donut Jesus,
You never answer me!
I am your biggest fan!
I am waiting to hear from you.
Please send me a letter
or your autograph
or some other sign.

I was at Chung King Lucky Noodle
when I finally got my answer.
My fortune cookie said:
CHANGE CAN ONLY COME FROM YOU.
Let's be fair. That was harsh.
I had to do this all by myself?
It took a while for this to sink in.
It took even longer for me to heal
from my breakup with Bad Boy Jesus.
But eventually,
I threw away all of my drawings of him,
and the love letters.
And I never went back to church again.

# The Rain Vacation

The language of water isn't spoken in these parts anymore.

The girl dreamed of what she had never seen –
drops falling from the sky,
trickles running down windowpanes,
beads hanging from branches like silver ornaments.
She dreamed of puddles,
and splashing in them in high boots.
She dreamed of water in gutters
and even of cars floating down the street.
She wanted to wear a raincoat and dreamed
of what she had seen in movies,
like *Singing in the Rain*, starring Gene Kelley.

Her parents remembered the rain
and wanted her to know it too.
So they took a rain vacation at a theme park:
Yellow slickers,
High boots,
Deep puddles,
Misting of water,
The Hurricane ride,
Salt water taffy,
The Soaker.
Water bagels.

The adults felt sad as they walked around the park.
Something they had taken for granted when they grew up,
something as ordinary as rain,
had vanished.
As they walked around the artificial place,
where you bought a ticket
for the tanks, hoses, and faucets,
they kept their sadness to themselves
because the children were squealing
and petting the water
like it was an extinct animal.

# The Smackdown

Maybe I should have saved all the money I spent on therapy
and invested it on one big
smackdown with my mother.
Ten rounds in the ring, last bitch standing.
I would make her beg for her breakfast
with my lightning-fast fists.

She is wearing red silk boxing shorts to match
her favorite red high-top sneakers.
Her t-shirt says I ♥ BEING A MOM
in rhinestone shit.
I am wearing black so I won't stand out.
Let her get the attention.
Let her get the applause when she opens
the ropes to step in.
The crowd applauds because
the skinny senior citizen is willing to fight.

When I step into the ring,
the crowd boos.
I am a bully.
I don't respect my elders.
I don't appreciate all she did for me.
That poor little old lady, giving birth
to a daughter like me.
What a shame.
But I don't really give a rat's ass what they think.
This isn't a court of law.
This is my chance to take her down.
My arms are tense with blood desire,
muscles tight from resisting the impulse
to clock her one in the jaw before the bell rings.
I want to punch her in that bitter mouth.
My jaw clenches.
I am hopping around on one foot and then the other.
I am sweating and nothing has started yet.

continued

I see people in the front row drinking beer
from tall-necked brown bottles.
I want a sip before the bell rings.
Heat rises from the crowd into the lights.

We come to the center of the ring,
a microphone drops from above,
the referee mumbles some rules,
I'm not paying attention.
A low growl begins in my throat.
When we tap our gloves, I feel a sizzle of electricity.
He says, "Go to your corners and come out fighting."
The bell rings.
I jump into the center of the ring.
My hands are in the defensive position
and my legs are loose.
I hear the growl again in my throat.
I want blood.
I am not afraid.
But then I see her scrawny legs--
stepping toward me in those stupid
red shoes.
I see what looks like fear in her eyes.
It's hard to be sure, I haven't seen that look before.
She isn't holding her gloves the right way.
I am circling her.
Then I have my chance –
the perfect opening for that easy punch to the mouth.
But my gloves are as heavy as boulders.
I look at her standing there, her eyes looking down,
gloves limp at her sides.
I notice that horseshoe-shaped scar on her knee –
she got it when she tripped over my Barbie and needed
12 stitches.
I stand there in the ring. I can't punch.
Her wrists look so vulnerable above the laced gloves.
Her forearms are chicken bones wrapped
in tissue paper.
And the fear thing in her eyes is getting worse.
She doesn't know what she's doing!

The first round bell hasn't rung yet
but I walk slowly back to my corner with
my head hanging low.
I crouch down there,
using my gloves as a pillow and I cry.
The referee holds my mother's hands up in victory.
The crowd goes wild!

# Dinner Rolls

You would not presume
that miniature Parker House rolls
would make good companions.
But, turns out,
they are well behaved and not lazy.
They are in fact good conversationalists,
very tidy,
have friendly personalities,
and are easy to travel with.

There was a fire once in our town
and while the smoke and ash rained down
on everyone else,
the fastidious little rolls
remained brave and perfect,
their buns fresh and buttery
until the flaky end.

# Fireworks

The kids, like the fireworks,
are ready to explode.
The old folks sit on hay bales applying
mosquito repellent.
The aerosol spray is oily
when rubbed on,
liquid citronella and cinnamon.

The names are too beautiful to burn:
Cracklers
Stone Roses
The Queen's Crown
Nest of Spiders
Azure Fountain
Monkey Machine.

Sparks, like escaped moths,
fly into the sycamore tree.
Red pebbles and blue stickers,
booms, pops, and the smell of punk.
Always one last sputter,
to leave the audience happy.

The kids are minotaurs,
half child, half adult.
They announce each beautiful name,
light it up and jump away.
Sometimes a flame remains
at the end,
a birthday candle that refuses
to be snuffed,
refuses to accept the added year.

Soon enough the kids will fly
like sparks,
to lives without us.
But tonight when I dream of them,
I am alight with happiness.
When I turn over in sleep,
my skin smells like
apple and citronella pie.

# Her First Word

Her first word was *material*.
The adults wondered why she skipped
all the warm-up words like *mama and daddy*.

So odd, they commented.
Why did *that* word emerge first
from the buttery spread of childhood?

Her home smelled like codfish balls and beer.
*The Mona Lisa*, torn from a magazine,
hung on a wall.

Pickpockets and drunks stopped by
while her uncle looked for coins on the sidewalk.
Her other uncle worked nights as a jailer.

He locked up family members as a joke.
Her grandmother had no teeth.
Her aunt thought Jell-0 was alive.

When the girl grew up, she seldom uttered
the word *material*. She did not build things or sew.
She lived simply and was not materialistic.

Maybe as a child she knew her family would provide
colorful material for her stories.
Maybe her first word was a warning to them to behave.

# If a Tree Falls

Multicolored lichen
grow up the legs of night.
My backpack is filled
with lint and stale biscuits.

Three times I call out,
Night, This Is Your Last Chance!
But there is no answer.

There is always a flame to walk toward.
There is always a hammer.
There is always the wind.

In dreams, I walk on a path
that sparkles in the moonlight.
In dreams my backpack is a cage of light.
In dreams, I call out to the night,
and it answers.

# Gardenias in My Tea

Except for a few words like *gracias* and *grande*,
I don't speak or understand Spanish.
This can be a disadvantage in Los Angeles where I live.
But on the other hand, where music is concerned,
ignorance can be bliss.

It is summer and I'm listening to lots of Cuban music.
I am also listening to Los Diamontes with their tight,
lush harmonies,
singing about,
well I have no idea.

I choose to think they are singing about the jungle at night.
Passionate love among the ferns.
Fiesta colored birds hanging like piñatas from the tall trees.
I choose to think the songs are about brown skin and soft lips
touching
under the fragrant flowers twisting up the vines.

In my ignorance,
It sounds like they are telling me my horse is on the tall mountain.
I think they are saying that in my trunk is a marble and some candles.
I think they say that I will wear my hat on Monday.
And I think they sing a lot about putting gardenias in my tea.

But I don't really care what they are saying.
I am happy to remain ignorant,
lost in the mysterious lyrics.
Lost in the jungle of sound
where I let myself drift away on the tropical breeze.
Where I will be wearing a tight white sarong,
and a red hibiscus in my hair
as I sip my gardenia tea.

# Dancing to Wagner

A swollen quartet
plays in the corner.
What does this night mean?
Wagner did not write tangos!
Yet here we are, trying to dance.

We are stuck on the verge,
the verge of what I cannot say.
We are stuck on this trivet of time.
We are dipping and sliding our feet.

Isn't this just like life?
We sought the liveliness
of a Latin dance,
a table by the stage,
small bites of Serrano ham.
Instead we are here
in this dark club
with its red velvet drapes,
at a table by the kitchen,
eating spaetzle.
Instead of a tango
we are stuck listening
to the Prozac thump of Wagner!

As we dance, our feet
shuffle from side to side.
We are dressed in our shiniest shoes,
and our socks with no holes.

As we dance, our eyes meet and hold.
Our lips touch.
Isn't this just like life?
Sometimes things can go so wrong
and still turn out so right.

# A Different Kind of Fire

There is an old love letter kind of fire.
There is a Thai chili on the tongue fire.
There is a marshmallow campfire fire.

Capture the image of me at nine in your mind.
See that girl with the hula hoop and the slinky?
On the back lawn in her cutoff shorts?
There was a flower appliqué on her pocket.

I remember your big hand in that pocket,
looking for a surprise, you said, your fat
fingers reaching down below, below, hurting me.

Let this be a warning to you!
If it ever happens again,
to another girl,
there will be a Burn Your House Down
With You In It, type of fire!

# Where Do Words Hang Out?

before they fall
like black blood
onto the white page?

Is there an organ sac,
a secret place like the soul or the spirit
where words ripen like zygotes?
Or are they born of a random synapse?

Once they become fledgling,
words can drift zigzag like leaves,
falling with a clatter,
a grunt, or a thump.

Where do words live
before they fall to the page?
And once they find the page,
where do they intend to go from there?

# A Hiccup in Time

I heard it on the radio yesterday.
Scientists have discovered a hole in time
filled with nature's hair and empty bottles.
I tried to follow along.
I imagined walking down a smooth street
and tripping on a lip of concrete –
(the scientists call this lip the event horizon).
Beneath this lip,
a black-mouthed sinkhole opens up –
blacker than the death of a dog.
The hole is infinite but the size of a pinprick –
expansive enough to contain a thousand black suns.
On the other side of the hole,
the sidewalk smooths out again.

Everything that falls into this hole disappears
into its mysterious depth:
baby shoes,
love letters,
arguments,
fold in on themselves –
scramble,
and become random particles
never to re-emerge.

The story made me feel very small.
Smaller than when I look up at the moon.
I realize I am a mere adhesion
on a thin tissue of time.
I am a postage stamp
on the missing envelope.
I am a floater,
a small pair of wings that forgot how to fly.
I am a cluster of pink buds falling,
into a gap of my own ignorance.

# The Pants

Your pants walked home without you.

Or maybe they ran home
like a dog spooked after thunder.

I don't know.

But I found the pants sitting on the porch,
one corduroy leg was crossed over the other.

I knew they were yours
by the corduroy itself and by the color.
It was of crushed gravel.
The catalogs would call it puma or pumice
or some other earthly and
non-descript thing.

I don't know.
But I knew they were yours
by the color and by the random paint stains.
Not like the stains that pretend-artists
splash on their clothes on purpose.
To make a pretend statement.
You don't need to make a statement.
It has been 45 years.
Your stains are earned.
Your stains are authentic.

"Where is he, boy?" I asked.
But the pants didn't answer because they were only pants.

"How do we get him to come home again?"

It was a prayer and a plea
and I asked it out loud,
right there on the front porch.
But the pants weren't talking.

# The New Mattress

There was an old woman who finally bought a new mattress.
Her old one had deep trenches dug into it.
No one could remember how old the mattress was
or how many husbands had died upon it.

On top of the new mattress, the old woman placed
a down comforter encased in a silken burgundy coverlet.
She walked by just to admire the beautiful sight.
She sighed when her hands caressed it.

In the first week, the old woman noticed some white fur
on the burgundy expanse, fur from her dog Louie.
To rectify this, she put a blue sheet over the burgundy coverlet.
While visually a disappointment, it kept it clean.

In a few more days, the old woman noticed some traces of mud
from Louie's feet on the blue sheet.
To rectify this, she put a floral picnic blanket over the sheet.
This subtracted from the sophistication, but kept it clean.

With the passage of time,
the old woman put sheets, towels, blankets,
coats, plastic bags, robes, tablecloths, and old clothing
on the bed to keep it free from dirt and fur.

When the coverings finally reached the ceiling,
and no dog or human could possibly reach it,
the old woman felt her bed was perfect,
and deemed it safe and clean at last.

# It's Better This Way

If you don't buy a house,
the hurricane can't destroy it.
If you don't adopt that rescue dog,
it will never get cancer
and go through all that treatment
just to vanish
as though you never had a dog in the first place.

When your boyfriend comes to pick you up
for the prom,
at the house you never owned,
don't worry.
Because then he won't
become your fiancé,
or later your husband.
He won't ever grow tired of you
and start dating his secretary,
which would lead to your divorcing him,
the husband you never married in the first place.
After the divorce, you would not bear his children,
children who would only grow up
needing therapy
because of the bad marriage you two never had.

One evening, the never husband would walk out the front door
of the house you didn't own.
The house that would have been washed away in the flooding
from that terrible hurricane.
So be grateful!
Count your blessings!

Believe me, it's better this way.

# A Solitary Leaf

See the wind?
It hovers over the water.
Animals wait at the gate.
Sometimes there are dumplings for them
and broth if it is cold.

Hear the wind?
It pulses in liquid distortion.
Sounds seem closer,
air blobs change their shape,
words from blocks away become screams,
but not really.

Smell the wind?
The perfume on the neck of the woman next door
blows over my fence.
It's like those inserts in magazines
that choke and sneeze the reader.

Where do I go in this wind?
The wind blows through my pores,
cleans me,
picks me up like a solitary leaf
and carries me to where the animals are.

I want to share blankets with them,
and dumplings, and broth,
because I am so cold on the inside.

# The Space Between Planets

We lay on his bed
looking at the planets
he had glued to the ceiling.

"I have some really important stuff
 never to tell you, I said.

"Secrets can be alive
 or dead," he said,
"or just asleep."

I had hoped he would care enough
to probe even a little for my secrets.

There was silence as I took in
the spicy smell
of his pet lizard.
On the bed with us were dirty socks,
wrinkled shirts,
and unopened mail.

"Your cat seems very healthy," I said.

# Eavesdropping on the Train

"I don't want to be part of a welfare type deal,"
the middle aged woman said to no one.
Her mouth was puckered with judgment,
"People on welfare should go to work
or clean up something if they want to be in this country."

She sat in the club car in her blue polyester pantsuit,
segregated from the rest of her tour group.
Her group shifted in their seats.
They glanced at each other.

"And they need to learn English if they want to stay here.
Why do we need to print *our* signs and ballots in *their* foreign
language?"

"Can you keep your voice down a little?" a man asked.
"I speak my mind, if you don't like what I'm saying, don't listen!
You *know* I'm telling the truth!"
The man excused himself and left.

"Oh look!" the woman said, pointing out the window,
"There's a lonely cow! Don't I know how *she* feels!"
She looked around.
"Maybe I should go talk to that cow!
Nobody in here's talkin' to me."
No one spoke.
"And *he* must be lonely," she said, twitching her head
toward the black bartender. "He has none of his own kind
here on the train to talk to."

"Look!" she pointed out the window.
"That pine tree is so straight!  As skinny
at the bottom as at the top! Just like a skinny girl with no chest.
The boys only go for the girls with big bosoms,
the loose ones, headed for trouble."

She seemed lost in thought. Her hair needed a touch up.
Her fingers traced the gray stripe down the center part
of her dark brown hair.
"My Alice was a sweet girl, a church girl. She was modest.
Her prom dress had a high neckline. She was gonna wear her
grandma's pearls. But she never made it to the prom.
Some drunk illegal hit her head-on. Some welfare cheat
with no insurance. Now I've got nothing.
No prom, no graduation, no wedding, no grand babies.
I try to keep busy.
I thought traveling would help."

"I need a refill," I said. "Can I get you something?"
She shook her head. I watched her from the bar,
her fingertips traveled mindlessly up and down
the gray median strip of her hair.
Maybe it divided her head into two lanes, I thought.
Grief on one side, anger on the other.

Coming back, she patted the seat next to her, an invitation.
I sat down.
The last of her tour group had gone.

The bartender lined up the glasses
and filled the bowls with nuts for the cocktail hour.
We sat in silence and watched
the light change out the window.
"I still hate those lazy welfare bums!" she whispered.
"I can't help it, I blame them. All of them."
It was dark before we knew it.

# Homecoming

I killed a spider today and I don't know why.
Usually, I take a paper towel
and ease it under the spider.
I fold him into the envelope and carry him outside
where I shake him into the purple sage plant.

I smile to myself,
imagining him entering his front door saying,
"Honey, I'm home!"
All the baby spiders
come running to him,
hairy legs outstretched in delight.

But not today.
Today I needed to take a bath.
Today, I was running late.
He was sitting in the strainer in the drain.
He was looking around and appeared content.
He wasn't causing any trouble.
He was just hanging out, being spiderly.

Today, he made me mad.
I was insulted.  I was put out.  I was offended.
Today it was all his fault.
It was his fault because . . .
I can't remember.

Today, I paid him back.
I flushed him into oblivion.
And because of me,
there will be no homecoming tonight
in the purple sage plant.

# Hotpants

"Those hotpants!" he said the night we met.
I stood there in the perfect silence of the lowlands,
looking at his slick teeth.
The flaps of grass were humming
as they waited for the fertility of spring.

I was a fool
to be entertaining thoughts
about a so-called deranged man
wearing a skeleton suit.
My grandma warned me about men
like him.

In the flaps of grass,
my pointy shoes aimed skyward
as the stars were strained through cheesecloth.
A scalpel had shaved his neck raw.
He smelled like pork rinds
and church candles
and Betty Crocker.

We lay in the field,
being eaten alive
by bitey-bugs,
biting
down there
where the hotpants
used to go.

# Entanglement Theory

You are there and I am here.
Your there is very far away.
My here is just the same old here.

There was an article in the paper yesterday about new research
on something they called entanglement theory.
In quantum mechanics of all things.
The theory demonstrates that two distant particles
can control each other
in ways that defy common physical sense.

In other words,
even if separated by thousands of miles,
when one particle says hello, the other particle waves
and says hello back.
Especially if the two particles were well acquainted
before the scientific separation took place.

I don't need to capture rubidium atoms in atom traps
and study them using elegant computerized models
to know how the experiment must end.
You must:
Turn in your Metro tickets,
Walk away from the Gruyere and the Louvre.
Pack your bags.
And come home, *s'il vous plait*,
to me,
your other particle.

# The Patron Saint

Santa Ana is the patron saint of cabinet makers,
horseback riders,
and unmarried mothers.
She becomes the patron saint of the insane
when her hot breath sweeps over Los Angeles.

The devil winds are rattling
the window panes of my soul.
They prickle my skin,
sending bolts of fire up my nose.
I am sneezing and itching,
my gums swelling like pink pillows.

As I walk the dogs at dawn,
dust swirls up the street searching out victims.
Wildfires blaze in the hills,
adding embers to
the Santa Ana cocktail –
bits of trees and homes,
plastic crumbs
and treasured documents,
are inhaled.

On a white wall
someone wrote in pencil:
Please Kill Me!
Walking further,
I see a new man living
near the onramp to the freeway.
He is wearing rags, living
in a pile of useless trash and chaos.
Yet on top of this mess,
is a clean wooden salad bowl
with two clean salad servers
crossed in the bowl like praying hands.

I can smell the sadness
on the stained fingers of the wind.

# Heart Bone

If there was a heart bone, it would have been buried too.
But the heart is a muscle, not a bone.

She would have buried it with the other bones
in order to sacrifice the child.
Perhaps she would have scattered the bones
in the oil fields
amidst the metal pumps
that stoop to sip the dust,
straighten and bend down
again and again.
Or she could have dropped the bones deep
in the fishing hole in the ice.
She would have sat dangling her fishing line
in that black hole
fishing for a visible sign,
as the snow stretched out on all sides of her
like the pregnant white belly of heaven.

The cheekbones would be buried first,
in order to snuff out all that excess smiling.
Next the entire pelvis would be buried,
though the specific use for it,
and the happiness it might have provided,
would not be understood for many years.

The femurs were laid down next,
laid deep down in the loamy soil,
to put an end to the running, skipping and hopping they did.

The finger bones were put to rest in a shallow grave
on a sheet of used Christmas gift-wrap
where they could no longer
untie ribbons
wave hello and goodbye,
hug strangers,
and pet kittens.

Once the burial was complete,
the useless child-parts continued to walk the earth:
the useless dust particles
the useless ice crystals
and of course the useless
and rusty heart bone
that, like the oil pumps in the field,
continued to bow
and eat dust
in order to survive.

# What the Famous Poet Taught Me

1.
The famous poet said
a poem is a breathing membrane,
a ventilation apparatus
that infuses each line with oxygen,
turning it from a naïve green
to a healthy newborn pink.

2.
The famous poet said
I should peck through the shell of a poem,
make blind progress
one word at a time,
until the stanzas glimpse daylight.

3.
The famous poet said
I should make the reader *want* to finish my poem.
I don't know what that means!
Today I read a poem that was shaped
like a balloon on the page!
Words trailing down
one at a time to form the string.
I could do that too!
Or maybe form a rocket ship or a heart.
How about offering the reader an incentive?
I could glue a quarter to the page
or embed a naked photo in the text?

4.
Turn over your card, the famous poet said,
don't be obscure, turn over your card.

# The Bears

I dreamed we saw a bear cub in Carol's house.
It was on the old Turkish carpet in the living room.
We were in the patio behind the screen doors.
There was oohing and pointing.
I as usual was the fearful one,
worried about the what-next.
Where there's a cub, I thought . . .
Sure enough,
a giant shadow rounded the corner
from the bedroom.
A behemoth she was,
all teeth and shag and grizz,
coming towards the flimsy
screen doors.

We could see the dirty pads of her paws
and her curved black nails
as she pushed on the wood around the screen.
We tried to hold her inside,
our shoulders straining to the job.
We pushed and pushed against
her mighty weight.
As the door splintered and blew open,
I woke up.

It was a reminder
that there is always a mother lurking behind everything.
You can't keep her away,
no matter how hard you push.

# Purple Summers

I met her in the river.
She was standing on the smooth stones,
afraid of the little nibble fish
that nipped and tickled her toes.
We were inseparable during those two summers.
When my parents found a mutant
apricot in the carton from the market,
they laughed and said it was us.
Two orange lumps,
melded together.

She wore the same purple bathing suit each summer.
It was rubbery and faded.
Each day,
more purple from her suit
washed downstream with the river water,
bumping over the big rocks,
cascading
down and down
to nowhere.

I noticed the bruises,
the color the bathing suit had once been,
on her arms and legs.
The bruises moved around her body
like a migrating flock of summer
birds under her skin.
As one faded from her arm,
a new bright one appeared on her thigh.
One day there was a big one on her throat.
Being only nine,
I didn't know how to ask her
about such things.

The third summer,
I jumped out of the car
and ran to the river,
expecting to see her standing there
waiting for me.
The smooth stones were empty
except for the little nibble fish
swimming around below
waiting for her toes.

I knew she wasn't coming back.
I paced up and down by the smooth stones,
looking for a part of her that I could keep forever.
A popsicle stick?
A purple thread from her bathing suit?
A candy wrapper?

Finding nothing,
I raced down the river,
past the smooth stones,
past the nibble fish,
past the big rocks,
past the waterfall cascade,
to the place where the water pooled.
There, I drank as much
as I could hold.
I needed to drink in the traces of her purpleness,
traces that had washed downstream
during those summers,
when we were together,
melded into one.

# Black Leather Memories

Give me your hand, my dear.
Stand on your shakes.
Steady yourself.
Pull your robe around you
and I will tie the belt.

Remember the boots you once wore?
The ones with the black leather fringe
and the hob nails?
Those boots were like two black arrows
pointing to what was hidden
under your skirt.
They were symbols of our youth,
of the nights when we danced
until your hair was wet.

Spring has come again, warm and mild.
Give me your hand, my dear.
Take a step. Then another.
We will walk to the door together
to greet the new morning.
Let's pretend you are wearing those boots
and that your hair is still wet from dancing.

# The Piñata

The children run at me with sticks,
their voices shrill, mouths set with fierce determination.

Before the first blow I hold my breath
and shift my paper eyes upward to the leaves and the sky.

I hang on the limb, a heavy fruit,
while the mothers stand around encouraging them to hit me harder.

The birthday cake is in the background,
but first, the slaughter.

I love the shy kids, the gentle ones who give me a tap, a pat.
They are more interested in the butterfly on the rose bush.

It's a living, but I often wonder
if I'm teaching them

that aggression wins, and that you have to whack the hell out of life
before you get to the sweetness within.

# Thanks for the Landfill

Salute your porridge!
Salute your zwieback too!
Praise for the one walnut
and for the tiered wedding cake!

Thanks for the night that returns
with such vigor and such regularity.
Thank you for the charred steak
that was barbequed on one such night
and for the mussels in their broth.

Thanks for the imposters,
the comedians,
and the exaggerators.
Thanks for the ones who tell
bad jokes. They need our forgiveness.

Thanks for big hairdos
and shiny bald heads.
Thanks for the little girl
with new hair ribbons
and for the little boy who just
applied his first hair gel.

Thanks for the landfill where we
bury our secrets.
Thanks for the palm frond hats
that peculiar members of the tribe wear.
Thanks for the stuffy newspapers
and for the zines printed on cheap paper.

Salute your thumbs!
Salute your bowl of beans too!
Praise for all the bad choices I have made,
because without them
I wouldn't be able to give thanks now.

# How Ignorant Bliss Is

When we first met,
I tried to tell you the truth about my secrets.
"I'm not normal," I said.
But you were too bewitched by lust to listen.

We kissed in candlelight,
our lips touched like tiny pillows.
Your hands caressed my face,
brushed the hair from my forehead.
Our eyes were deep tunnels that travelled
to a destination we would figure out later.

Then, like all the others, your fingers
reached for the button on my blouse.
Then you loosened the second button.
With the third, my secret was revealed.
Your focus at first was on the crème lace underneath,
on the invitation between my breasts.

Then your eyes stopped on my feathery torso,
feathers that sprouted from all my secret places.
Your eyes, like all the others, were accusing.
My feathers stirred and caught the candlelight,
their tips brushed with blonde fire.
My feathers shivered in the breeze from the window.

"I told you I wasn't normal," I said.
Contempt filled your eyes
as I rose from the bed
climbed onto the sill
and flew away.

# Family History with Birds, Molasses and Jesus

*Women are like an empty birdcage.*

*— my father*

When my mother died, I gave away
her antique birdcage.
It was made of white wicker
and had elaborate spaces for birds to roam.
Like my mother, nothing ever lived inside,
and like my mother, the surface was decorated
with fancies and curlicues
designed to entice a mate.

*Men are slow as molasses.*

*— my mother*

The man sits and waits. La-de-dah, he thinks. No rush.
He ponders.
He examines his beard in the mirror.
He whistles a tuneless melody.
He watches the traffic go by.
He watches golf on TV.
He admires his collection of ties.
He snacks on cheese.

*Jesus wept.*

*— my brother*

"It's raining in Portland," my brother says.
"What is rain?" I say. "I've heard of it."
"Rain is God crying," he says.
"He must be overjoyed with Los Angeles then," I say.
"Yes! He likes you guys a lot! He gave you the best
Mexican food."
"I think he would be a burrito kind of guy,
beans and cheese, no meat. He loves animals too much."
"I think he would order nachos and a tamarind horchata,"
my brother says.

My brother lives in Portland where it rains a lot.
I live in Los Angeles where it doesn't.
My brother's favorite expletive is Jesus Wept.
"Jesus Wept," he says when we talk about my mother,
the empty birdcage,
or my father who is brown and slow like molasses.

# The Creditors

On the patio, only my lawn chair remains.
The other furniture was sold at auction.

My neighbor, the shapely one with the great legs,
is out on her patio pruning roses.
She's wearing headphones and between snips,
she twirls and raises her arm straight up
into the air like a disco queen.
I imagine her perfect life.
She has things to do.
She has things to look forward to.
She is making a contribution.

It's been a few days since I wore real clothes
and not this bathrobe that was his.
The red plaid is like a soft ghost
I don't want to remove.

I stare at my neighbor,
her flat midriff,
her energy.
Later she will probably go to the gym,
then dinner and a movie.

All I have
to look forward to are the telephone calls
from the creditors.
I welcome the silence or the gasp
when they ask for him
and I say he can't come to the phone right now,
he's dead.

# Miracle on Stanford Street

I was whelped in San Diego,
then carried home in a dresser drawer
padded with a motel towel.
My body smelled of cheap pine and glue.

As a child I believed my eyes were cameras.
I believed that even though no one listened to me
in my house on Stanford Street,

my devoted audience would eagerly
tune in to my TV show called Handy Hints
and learn everything I knew.

My Handy Hints included how to make orange juice
from crushed flowers
and how to skip rope wearing roller skates.

At night, I listened to boxing matches in bed,
my ear pressed to the green transistor radio,
the announcer yelling

that one huge animal had knocked out another,
while I, the little magpie,
gathered the fighting words

like blue threads,
to stitch together
a grand life I didn't know.

# The Big Winner

At night, I sometimes sneak up on my own house
pretending to be a stranger.
Who lives in there, I wonder?
What are they really like?
Are they happy?
Do they understand life?
Through the side window of the living room,
I see two dogs curled on the couch,
waiting for the shake of dry kibbles.
From this side, I hear the neighbor's TV,
people cheering on a game show,
clever players vying to win big prizes.

Through the open window, I can smell my house:
dog fur, flowers, and dust.
I also smell the spaghetti sauce simmering. . .
My glasses lie on the kitchen counter
next to the defrosting bag of peas.
I think my phone is ringing in the back of the house.
The lamp on the piano casts
a mellow light on the old wood
of the upright Chickering.
I remember how my husband
started taking piano lessons at 40
and the beginner piece he practiced –
for hours – made me want to run away.

He will swing into the driveway soon
and I will call yoo-hoo to him from the kitchen.
I will be standing by the stove stirring the sauce
and sipping a glass of  red wine.
He will give me a hug and a kiss
and ask what's for dinner.
While he's greeting the dogs on the couch,
I'll pour out the kibbles.
I'll put the peas in the microwave,
reach for the pasta bowls
and the grated cheese.

Later he might play me the new
Chopin nocturne he just learned.

# This Is a Poem Holding Its Breath

This is my foot on Billy's floor.
This is the rosemary sprig I stole from the bush
because smelling it prevents Alzheimer's.
This is the poem I tried to find on the train.

This is Lloyd's nose on my pants
and this is the smudge he leaves.
This is a picture of dad and me in Maui.
I'm wearing a black bathing suit
and Dad is wearing a straw hat.
This is SpongeBob on TV.
This is Liverpool kicking the ball across the grass.
This is cheese and crackers on a plate I remember.
This is sliced tomatoes from the yard.
This is a blank where I forget the words.
This is me smelling the rosemary again.

What happened to dad's straw hat?
What happened to it when we cleaned out his house?
I hope someone is wearing it in Maui,
watching the sunset like we used to do.
Or maybe someone
will find his hat when they clean out my house?

# The Silver Bullet

I can't talk about the bear.
But images of him, big and brown, keep coming.
I picture his innocent eyes, stunned,
as he stepped from behind the trees.

The freight train was nearly two miles long
and full of supplies.
Maybe it was carrying garden furniture,
or pallets of beer from Portland.
Maybe it carried redwood for fancy
home improvements.

The bear carried nothing at all,
just his brown fur,
and perhaps a dream of fall,
the leaves yellow and crisp,
the sap humming behind the bark.
Maybe he was admiring the midnight sky
and the splash of silver stars.
The leftover harvest moon was shining on him
when he stepped out from the trees.

I can't talk about the bear anymore.
But I hope he was looking at a falling moonbeam
when it happened.

# Oh, Thank Heaven

The sun will rise in two hours.
I walk the dogs through the dark morning
toward Ballona Creeek, my pretend river.
There is new graffiti I can't decipher,
and a balloon face wearing a smile.
In the lumberyard stand two bears,
adult and child, carved out of logs,
and the beheaded palm trees wearing hula skirts.

On the corner glows my oasis, the convenience store.
Light spills onto the broken concrete like hot lemon topping.
I can see the cardboard cups, their butts toward me,
sleeping in their burrows, small, medium and large.
Above their heads, pots of coffee brew.
Racks of candy and colorful magazines line the walls.
Breakfast sandwiches and hotdogs warm in the steamer.

Standing behind the counter in his maroon vest is the clerk.
Today he looks at his phone.
Sometimes he cleans the windows.
Sometimes he sweeps the floor.
Sometimes he restocks the shelves.
I imagine him waving to me as I pass.
I imagine him coming to the doorway
to say, "Good morning neighbor! Come on in, it's warm!"

# Surfing in Bangalore

Tomorrow I will be on my way to meet my bride.
The one my parents chose for me.
The one I have never met.
The one I have never even seen
except in a blurry photograph.

In the meantime,
I'm working on my surfboard
in the backyard of our house in
Torrance, California.
The summer sun is beating down hard
on my bare back and arms.
I'm barefoot and wearing my orange surfing shorts
the ones with the Hawaiian flower print.
Fall will be here soon and it is
rustling around the edges of the yard
like a whispered secret.

I'm applying the small squares of
fiberglass fabric
to the dings on the board.
After that, I will cover each one with resin
and sand the patches smooth.
The last step will be to apply the wax.
I'll never forget the smell of the wax
when it's mixed with salt from the ocean
and baked by the summer sun.

While I'm sanding, I glance around the yard
so I can remember everything.
The garage door I painted green with my dad.
The cracks in the driveway.
The gap in the tree where the rotten limb
I was climbing on broke away.
Saber's squeaky dog toy lying in the grass.
My bedroom window with the view of the lemon tree.

Once I get to Bangalore
and marry the stranger,
I plan on removing the heavy red and gold wedding garments,
the jewelry,
and the makeup.
I will change
into my orange surfing shorts
and flip flops.
I will walk over to Ulsoor Lake,
the only body of water in Bangalore.
There I will sit under a tree by the side of the lake
and sing all the songs I know
by The Beach Boys.

# Dark Stains

Like an unpopped kernel of corn,
like a lost mitten,
like a closet without a hanger,
death is just so *ordinary*.

Think of death as a final meal.
Enjoy the appetizer!
Think of the first bites
as a beginning,
not the beginning of the end.

Think of the meal
as a summary of your life.
Dig your spoon into the broth,
taste the bitter brine,
the sugary, the sour.

Taste the scrape and the crunchy.
Taste the puffed and the whipped.
Oh the saltines! Lick your spoon!
Take a picture of your perfect plate.

Like a journal without a word,
like a rusty nail in a wall,
like an infant's unwrapped clothes,
death is just so *ordinary*.

# Freesia in Winter

Trouble can't find me here.
Stars, the dogs of ice,
shine down on the smooth
blackness of my earthen bed.
Muffled by dirt, I hold my breath,
waiting for a change.

Shivering in my brown fur overcoat,
and my sprouted night cap,
I wait like a mole.
I have no vision.
Is anyone there?

Tendrils of root reach out
like a blind man reaches out
with his white cane.

The rain falls like big shoes
walking overhead.
I am a cemetery.
I survive on earthworms,
bits of shell and remembered songs.

I wait for change.
Was that warmth?
Was that light?
Was that birdsong?

At last I push aside
my coverlet of leaves
and stretch my stems,
stretching them to the sun.
Soon there will be a celebration,
a homecoming.

In appreciation,
I will bring fragrant white
blossoms to share.

# The Candelabra

After dark, her torso glints
under the candelabra.
Small lights,
those pretend candles of glass,
flicker and share the secrets of her skin.

With the Braille of my fingers,
I awaken the sleeping birds.
They flutter from their confinement
like giddy children on the playground,
running and flapping their wings.

# Ungirdle My Loins

I am the clock unwinder,
the bell unringer.
I remove the smut from smitten.

I am the clothing shrinker,
the hope dasher.
I remove the de from delight.

I am the corn unpopper,
the soufflé flattener.
I remove the luxe from deluxe.

I am the hair tangler,
the zipper snagger.
I remove the glee from gleeful.

Now, with time running short,
I'm making adjustments.
I'm working to put
the gravitas back into gravlax.

# The New Toaster

I had to buy a new toaster.
The old one was too slow.
And it didn't have big enough slots
for oversized muffins and bagels.
The new one is all white plastic and chrome.
Confident, fast, and a four-seater.

I hate it.
It will most likely outlive me.

I hate it because it flaunts its youth and beauty.
Right in my face,
it smirks at me with its metallic grin.
I think it throws parties late at night in that tight white skirt,
its lewd mouth open, probably laughing at some racy joke
while serving buttered toast to the drunken guests.

But mostly I hate it
because it will probably outlive me.
And it will live on to fix muffins and bagels
for my family on Christmas morning.
As though I am as easy to replace
as an old, broken-down toaster.

# Champagne

When all the stars fall
from the sky into my glass,
I know I am drinking champagne.

While sipping the galaxy,
my hair becomes soft again and long.
And it becomes its natural auburn color,
instead of this chemical red hat that I wear nowadays.

While sipping the galaxy,
music sounds miraculous and new.
I am listening to Los Diamontes on the jukebox.
They are singing boleros about finding love on the road.
Their name,
Los Diamontes, means
The Diamonds
if my elementary Spanish holds.
Diamonds are similar to the chipped stars floating in my glass.

While drinking stars from the galaxy,
my neck becomes smooth again,
and there is a chance that the man on the stool across from me
is actually looking at me
instead of the bar clock
hanging on the wall.
The one behind my head
that shows how many minutes remain
until closing time.

# Why I Hate Halloween

Apples make me sad.
Snow White almost died from eating one.
Fall is such a stern season.

Halloween is a time for the tragic,
the sick and the decayed
to stagger around scaring people.

They jump from behind walls
and we are supposed to laugh.
The bigger the scare the bigger the laugh.

Candy can be poisoned like apples.
Blood drips down faces, but this isn't really funny.
Teeth are sharp and can bite the unsuspecting neck.

Dinge and gore stare at us with infected eyes.
Scars are mocked.
Pumpkins pretend to be mentally ill.
Beautiful girls are made ugly

and handsome boys are made fearsome.
Limps are faked, timid voices scream,
and unflattering orange is worn far too often.

I wish happiness itself would
jump out from behind that hedge near my porch.
I wish happiness itself would put its musty-smelling
hands over my mouth.

I wish happiness itself would bite my neck
and let my bad blood flow.
I wish happiness itself would cackle
and throw me to the ground
and have its way with me.

# Goldfish

My heart is thinking about the dream of the goldfish.
They were swimming in the old suitcase.
The one I travelled with
to a convention in Philadelphia.

When I got to the hotel, I realized the water level
in the suitcase was dangerously low.
I refilled it from the bathtub,
but the fish overflowed, washing over the side.
I lost them in the shag carpet, the color of pumpkin pie.

On my knees, weeping,
I searched among the wet strands.
I combed the orange seaweed with my fingers
and called "please come back."

I know the dream is about you.
Like the fish, you are flopping around,
lost in the wet strands of your bad decisions.

You rest lightly upon this earth.
Your roots are not deep.
Your mouth opens and closes,
forming empty vowels.

You always wanted me to write about you.
Sorry. This might not be what you hoped for,
being compared to goldfish
gasping for breath on an old orange carpet.

# Oh, Irksome One

We are together again.
I met him back when his hair was brown,
when he still had eyebrows,
had no need for glasses.

He is here washing under his arms
in the basin we once found at the thrift store.
The hot water flows into it.
The basin is chipped now, it was new then.
The wind scratches at our window.

He came back from cavorting
with the Sirens. They beckoned to him
from their rocks while he was lost at sea,
floating with the current,
no stability in sight.

We are together again
in the old house.
Soon the night will unfasten itself.
In the fireplace, we will toast bread on forks.
We will drink our glasses of wine.

I don't mind his gray hair
his bad teeth,
the unwashed smell of him.
I don't even mind him being irksome.
If only he would say he's sorry,

# The Zebras

She wants to trace the stripes with her fingertips
to the terminus, like Braille or a map.

She wants to dream of them,
spy on them,
tickle them while they sleep.

"Just a peek beyond the chain-link fence,"
she tells herself on that hazy morning.

The zebras dip their muzzles into the water trough
and pull up quickly. Bubbles rise to the surface.

She wants to know the wilderness of their fur,
taste the bubbles from the trough with her lips.

She wants them to accept her into their dazzle
and not be afraid.

The zebras smell her
before they see her –
the pink shoes pushed into the toe holds of the fence.

# Silvercoat

If I am hungry, I can eat words.
I learned that last night in a dream.
I could feel the scratch of the Z and the W
as they went down my throat.

Words nourish me,
like when Anthony Doerr describes
young Marie eating canned peaches:
"She's eating wedges of wet sunlight," he writes.

Those are edible words!
But the ocean, not words,
provides my nourishment.

From birth, I lived five blocks
from the edge of the sea.
The ocean held me aloft, showed me off.
my rolling womb, my frolic room.

I swam amidst the bulbous tubes.
Like arms, they reached for me,
petted me. The waves cradled me,
left salt on my skin,
my silvercoat,
the placenta of my true birth mother.

# My Mind Wanders

out the door every night,
wearing sensible shoes,
carrying only a phone.

My mind wanders
past the spice factory
with the steel vats,
past the hamburger stand
that sells firewood,
past the place that collects metal husks
of cars killed in accidents.

I read a joke today that said,
"I think senility will be a smooth transition for me."

Maybe what really happens
is that the mind wanders.
It travels, for instance,
to the Galapagos to be with the turtles.
Or maybe to the Shamishiri Forest
where it watches a bird on a treetop
sip milk from the moon.

Maybe it's not senility at all.
Maybe the mind just wanders.
And maybe it's so engrossed
in what it sees,
it forgets to come home.

# What I Learned This Morning

I can't sleep.
It is hours until dawn
and I'm watching TV.
The green numerals on the bedside clock
say 3:15.

The programs on TV are either infomercials
or re-runs of old crime dramas.

So far, I have learned
my pores are clogged.
My vagina has an unpleasant odor.
My carpet, clean to *my* untrained eye,
is filled with trapped dirt.
I can lose 30 lbs. in a month by
wearing a magnetic belt.
I can lose another 30 lbs. in a month by
taking mega-vitamins.
I need to jazz up my sex life
before my husband strays.
My teeth are yellow.
My hair is flat and unattractive
and can be fixed by using
a special contour brush.
My makeup is all wrong and I can look
years younger by using a spray airbrush device.

I turn to the crime drama.
A domestic abuse victim is on the stand
being questioned by the defense attorney:
"Why didn't you just move out?" he asks her.
"Why would you choose to remain in
an abusive relationship?
Where was your self-esteem?"

If he had ever watched early morning TV,
he would know the answer:
Women are defective and always wrong.
So they deserve what they get.

# Chimpanzee Mind

The chimpanzee and I sat
in the United Airlines boarding area.
We were waiting to catch
the same flight.
His little hairy legs hung down
over the edge of the plastic seat,
not quite reaching the floor.
He wasn't dressed in a costume,
or eating,
or drinking coffee,
or reading a magazine.
He just sat there
staring off into middle space,
watching people.

I wondered
what he was thinking.
Was he preparing for some comedy routine?
Was he going to blast off into space?
Was he going to be tested for science?

Maybe he was watching me!
Maybe he was wondering
what *I* was thinking.
Why I looked so sad, for instance.
Or where I was going by myself.
Or why I wasn't wearing a wedding ring.

# Wanderlust

Yes, but where would I go?

Overland doesn't appeal to me,
too many mushrooms.
Too many poor farmers pushing on their plows.

The sea doesn't appeal to me,
too much immersion and splash.
Too many seaweed tangles touching the foot.

The air doesn't appeal to me either,
the false night banging on the windows.
Too many herring sandwiches.

Inside all of us is a pill bug curled
in on itself, little feelers tucked away
under the rollie-pollie contour.
An accordion pleated backbone
protecting the tender heart beneath.

Don't be afraid!
Beckon the drums why don't you?
How about some streamers?
Button up your tanzer coat and
pull on your tackety boots.
Life is here for us to devour!
We just have to figure out where to go.

# Prayers and Dustpan

Sippy cups and butt jokes are in the past.
The kids have moved on to being cool,
wearing hoodies in the house and giving one word answers.
The adults follow them into adolescence
with prayers and a dustpan.

The table is littered with dirty dishes.
A few sourdough rolls remain in the basket.
The women are waiting for the men to get a clue,
clear the table, and put the dishes in the dishwasher.

The kids are sprawled on couches and chairs,
looking at their iPhones and game devices.
One of the adults mentions Man Ray,
the American surrealist.

Another adult says,
"Have you heard of his son Gamma Ray?"
Young eyes raise to the ceiling,
reentering from electronic-land.
It's communion, like papal smoke, wafting in.

One kid says, "Yeah, I heard he has a kid named Sting Ray."
Another adds, "And one named X."
Like a kinked hose letting loose,
the room is sprayed with the sweet benediction of laughter
and for a moment we are all together again.

# ACKNOWLEDGMENTS

Grateful acknowledgment is made to the editors of the following publications in which some of these poems have appeared:

Forge
Atlanta Review
Crack The Spine
Lummox Journal
The Louisville Review
Found Poetry Review
Burningword Literary Journal
Blue Lake Review
G.W. Review
Reed Magazine
Permafrost
Mas Tequila Review
The Round
The Griffin
Sanskrit
Foliate Oak
Talking River
Organs of Vision and Speech Literary Magazine
Willow Review
The Tower Journal
Chaparral
Poetry Super Highway
Kind Of A Hurricane Press
Knot Literary Magazine
Thin Air Magazine

Fre&d
The Manhattanville Review
poeticdiversity
The Evansville Review
Serving House Journal
Silver Birch Press
Schuylkill Valley Journal
Licking River Review
San Diego Poetry Annual
Chiron Review
The Hollins Critic
Pamplemousse
Burningword Literary Journal
Long Limbs Creative
Spectrum Publishing

# THANKS

Thank you to my family:
    Bill and Rhonda Reedy, Carol Blake,
    Trish and Eddie Field, Geoffrey and Alison Hale
    and Richard Hale.

Special thanks and love to Franie, Josh, Maddie, and Max.

Thank you to my clients for their courage, their open hearts
and for all they taught me.

Love to my guardian angel Barbara Hopkins Dorough Smith.

Thank you to Jack Grapes, Tom Brod, Alexis Rhone Fancher
    and The Gaman Writer's Collective.

Love and blessings to Jess Fritz. I am inspired by who you are.

# CREDITS

**Front Cover:** untitled
— MATT ADRIAN, 2015
*The Mincing Mockingbird*
mattadrian.com

**Back Cover:** ALEXIS RHONE FANCHER

**Page 95:** BAZ HERE

# ABOUT THE POET

Born in Santa Monica to a tennis champion (her father won the 1942 U.S. Hard Court Doubles title with Billy Talbert) and a homemaker who wanted to be French (her mother), **Suzanne O'Connell** put herself through college as a senior clerk typist. She earned her degree in social work from UCLA.

Seeking adventure, she became a mental health disaster volunteer. In pursuit of further adventure, she became a poet.

Nominated for a Pushcart Prize and for Best of the Net (2015), her work has been widely published in literary and poetry journals and magazines. (suzanneoconnell-poet.com)

This is her first collection of poems.

Made in the USA
San Bernardino, CA
11 April 2016